# The Un-Wily Hare

by Hertha James

## A Storybook for You to Illustrate

Powerword Publications

herthamuddyhorse@gmail.com

hertha.james@xtra.co.nz

Copyright © text 2023 Hertha James



Each book in the series,
***For Budding Artists and Illustrators,***
has nine pages of text and a blank page alongside for the artist.

Edited by Bonnie Boon
Cover, title page, p 24 graphics by Hertha James
Page 5 photo of Big Boy and Fred by Margaret Gurr

ISBN 978-1-7385915-5-8

## USING THIS BOOK

The book has a blank page for illustration alongside each page of text, and additional space for the artist on the text pages.

The idea is to have fun with any drawing style(s) that you like or want to practice.

The paper is not suitable for watercolour or felt pen. Pencil, colored pencils, charcoal pencils, wax crayons, pastels, and ink will work nicely.

Your focus might be stick figures, faces with expressions, clothing/fashion, cartoon drawing, closeups or wider scenes, bird's eye view, caricature, photorealism,

You may want to practice quick sketching, line drawing, doodling, figure drawing, gesture drawing, perspective.

You may want to play with shading techniques (hatching, stippling, scribbling, smudging) to create shadow, texture, and blending.

You may want to draw digitally, print out, and glue into the book.

You could find, or set up, scenes to photograph, print out, and paste into the book.

**The series includes these titles:**

*Jack Defrosting* is a humorous tale about a boy who must solve a dilemma. Suitable for reluctant readers.

*Mystery of the Garden Gnomes* tells the story of a garden brought back to life.

*Bad Baby Bear* is a retelling of 'Goldilocks and the Three Bears' from the Baby Bear's point of view.

*Cindy* is a modernized re-telling of 'Cinderella'.

*Slip Sliding Away* takes us through a trauma brought on by global warming.

*Boo the Rescue Greyhound* is about a girl who is excited to adopt a dog. She trains the dog well and they help solve a mystery.

*The Cow Shows How* is a story about how a girl overcomes her fear of giving a speech to her English class.

*The Un-Wily Hare* (this book) is a re-telling of 'The Tortoise and the Hare' story in the real world, almost.

*Worm Rescue* is a true story about distressed earthworms collected and given a new garden home.

**Look out for more titles to come.**

For my father who loved animals of all kinds and
who let me have a monkey.

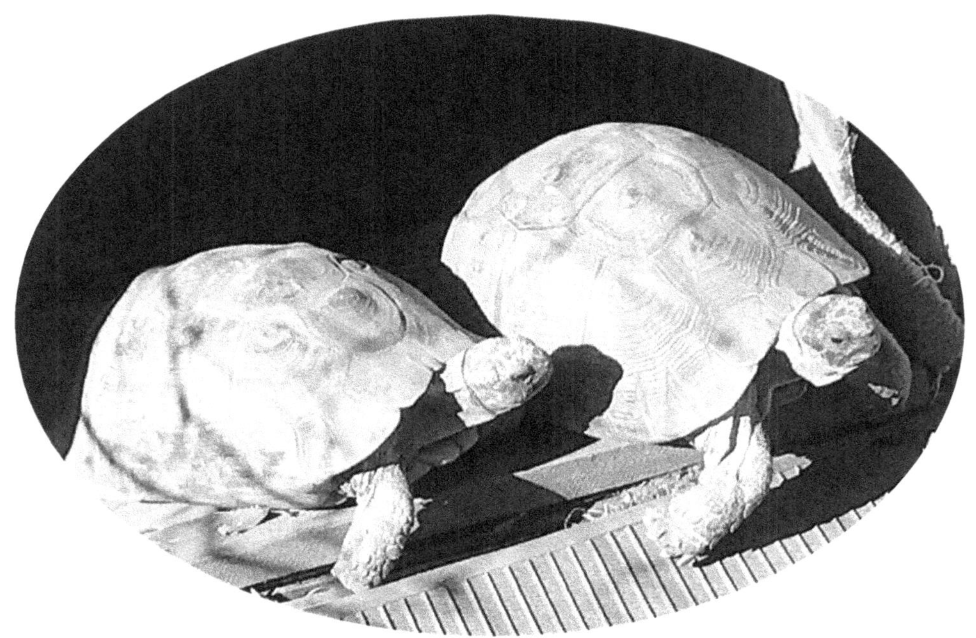

# The Un-Wily Hare

Tortoise was sound asleep in a thick clump of grass. His friend, Hare, was in the meadow nibbling the freshest bits of grass he could find. He was always hungry.

Bob Blackbird swooped in to sit on the branch of a nearby tree. "Have you heard?" he asked. "The strawberries are ripe, and the farmer has taken the covers off for the pickers."

Tortoise felt his lips pucker at the thought of those delicious, juicy strawberries. He would have to hurry to get there in time before the netting was put back for the night.

Hare hopped over. He was excited about the news too. Strawberries were a rare luxury.

"It's a long way to go," Tortoise sighed. "I guess I'd better get going."

Bob Blackbird cackled in the tree. "I have a bet on Tortoise getting there before you, Hare," he said. "You're always distracted by something. I have a bet with two Blackbirds who don't believe me. They think that you will easily beat Tortoise to the strawberries."

Hare stretched and yawned. "You'll lose your bet, you silly Blackbird."

Tortoise clambered out of his comfortable grassy nest. He used the sun to set the right direction across the pasture. He liked to take the shortest route to any destination.

Hare watched him, twitching his nose. Tortoise always amused him. He was so set in his ways. He did the same thing over and over again. Every day.

Hare liked variety in his day. He hopped here. He hopped there. He liked to tease the fat little dog on the farm. He played with his hare friends. He gossiped with the ducks.

He watched for the hawks in the sky and told the ducklings when to hide. He snuck into the farmer's garden to nibble the vegetables. He especially liked to snack on newly planted trees.

Hare watched Tortoise amble off until he was out of sight. Then he crept into the cosy nest Tortoise had made in the big clump of grass and had a long, refreshing snooze.

Meanwhile, a fox spotted Tortoise making his way to the strawberry field. He hid in the bushes watching him approach. As Tortoise walked by, the fox jumped on him.

Tortoise drew his head, feet, and tail tightly inside his shell. The fox prodded and poked at him. The fox tried to turn him upside-down.

But Tortoise was too heavy for this. Then the fox tried to nudge him along to roll him down a bank. Finally, the fox gave up and trotted away.

Tortoise cautiously pushed his head out of his shell to look around. All seemed clear. He pushed out his feet and tail, set his course again, and continued his journey to the strawberry field.

Meanwhile, Hare woke up from his deep sleep. He checked to see where the sun was.

"Oh my. It's much later than I thought.
A Blackbird should have come around
and woken me up. I can't let Tortoise get
there first. I'd never hear the end of it."

Hare knew a shortcut to the
strawberry field. He hopped along at a
leisurely pace. Catching up with Tortoise
was just too easy.

The fox was resting in the shadow of
a big tree. Chasing hares was good sport.
If he was lucky, he could end up with his
dinner sorted. He waited motionless
until Hare was close.

The fox jumped out. Startled, Hare
leapt into the air, turning 180 degrees to
confuse the fox. Then he ran as fast as
he could.

The fox followed. He knew where Hare would try to hide and set his course to cut him off.

Then, to Hare's dismay, another fox joined the chase.

Hare realized that he would not be able to outsmart two foxes. He could easily outrun one fox. But two foxes made life difficult. His only hope was to get to the farmer's woodpile. He knew a way to squeeze into the woodpile so foxes couldn't reach him.

But that woodpile was a long way, and in the opposite direction of the strawberry field.

Hare was breathing hard. His heart thumped loudly. Would he make it?

He changed direction and ran a zig-zag course to the farmyard. He hoped the big dog was not around.

It was good fun to tease the little fat dog, but the big dog was scary.

He could see the woodpile in the distance. He leaped across a stream and dodged between trees.

One fox was behind him and the other was to the side, trying to cut him off from the woodpile.

Hare flew through the farmyard, whooshed through the panels of a wooden fence and dived into his safe hiding place.

Eventually the foxes grew weary of sniffing around the woodpile and wandered off.

When Hare was sure they were gone, he crawled out and stretched his stiff muscles. He sniffed the air for any hint of the big farm dog.

It felt safe, so he stiffly loped off in the direction of the strawberry field. The sun was drooping in the west.

He met Tortoise starting on his way back from the strawberry field. His chin was stained red with strawberry juice.

"Where have you been?" asked Tortoise. The Blackbirds have been arguing for an hour about whether you would show up at all. The strawberries are all covered up again, but Bob Blackbird dropped some under a tree for you when he won his bet, in case you finally got here.

"Long story," said Hare.

"Let's find a place to rest," said Tortoise. "I'm stuffed full of strawberries, and you look all worn out."

# ABOUT THE AUTHOR

Hertha James is the author of sixteen books about training horses with positive reinforcement, available via Amazon.

After a career as a zookeeper and animal handler on film sets, she taught high school Science and Biology for many years.

Her writing also includes:

- Extensive write-on resources for learning science vocabulary, which are highly popular in many schools.
- For young readers, a four-book series featuring horses published by Pinnacle Press.
- A series of three books introducing students to working in a science lab, published by Essential Resources.

*The author with two young cougars during her film-making career..*

www.ingramcontent.com/pod-product-compliance
Lightning Source LLC
Chambersburg PA
CBHW080508030726
47592CB00011B/3296